GET TO WORK!

PLANNING TO BUILD WITH AN ARCHITECT

BY JOAN STOLTMAN

Gareth Stevens PUBLISHING

Please visit our website, www.garethstevens.com. For a free color catalog of all our high-quality books, call toll free 1-800-542-2595 or fax 1-877-542-2596.

Library of Congress Cataloging-in-Publication Data

Names: Stoltman, Joan, author.
Title: Planning to build with an architect / Joan Stoltman.
Description: New York : Gareth Stevens Publishing, 2019. | Series: Get to work! | Includes bibliographical references and index.
Identifiers: LCCN 2017025324| ISBN 9781538212370 (pbk.) | ISBN 9781538212387 (6 pack) | ISBN 9781538215791 (library bound)
Subjects: LCSH: Architects–Juvenile literature. | Architecture–Vocational guidance–Juvenile literature.
Classification: LCC NA1995 .S76 2018 | DDC 720.92–dc23
LC record available at https://lccn.loc.gov/2017025324

Published in 2019 by
Gareth Stevens Publishing
111 East 14th Street, Suite 349
New York, NY 10003

Designer: Bethany Perl
Editor: Joan Stoltman

Photo credits: Cover, p. 1 (architect) Rawpixel/Shutterstock.com; pp. 1-24 (background) MaLija/Shutterstock.com; pp. 1-24 (rectangular banner) punsayaporn/Shutterstock.com; pp. 1-24 (blueprint background) Marsan/Shutterstock.com; p. 5 (main) Sxenko/Wikipedia.org; p. 5 (inset) Al Ravenna/New York World-Telegram and Sun/Wikipedia.org; p. 7 (model) Nicholas Cope/Stone/Getty Images; p. 7 (blueprint) Dr Project/Shutterstock.com; pp. 8-16 (text box) LoveVectorGirl/Shutterstock.com; p. 9 Vincenzo De Bernardo/Shutterstock.com; pp. 11, 21 (graph paper) inxti/Shutterstock.com; p. 11 (elevations) Nadezhda Shuparskaia/Shutterstock.com; p. 13 (large kitchen) Breadmaker/Shutterstock.com; p. 13 (small kitchen) Cinematographer/Shutterstock.com; p. 15 pritsana/Shutterstock.com; p. 17 miker/Shutterstock.com; p. 19 Morsa Images/DigitalVision/Getty Images; p. 21 (floorplan) Martina Vaculikova/Shutterstock.com; p. 21 (elevation) Tasiania/Shutterstock.com; p. 21 (torn paper and tape) Flas100/Shutterstock.com.

Printed in the United States of America

CPSIA compliance information: Batch #CS18GS: For further information contact Gareth Stevens, New York, New York at 1-800-542-2595.

CONTENTS

Words in the glossary appear in **bold** type the first time they are used in the text.

ARCHITECTURE AND ARCHITECTS

We all need places to live, learn, work, shop, and eat, right? The **environment** around you includes everything from furniture to **landscaping**. Even small buildings are first **designed** and then built—and so are big cities! Architects design all these parts of your world!

Architects practice the science, art, and business of designing buildings in all forms. Their field is known as architecture. They're **responsible** for designing buildings and spaces. After designing, an architect is responsible for planning and overseeing the construction.

FRANK LLOYD WRIGHT

Architect Frank Lloyd Wright designed this Pennsylvania home called Fallingwater in 1935. It's one of the most famous buildings in the world!

ON THE JOB

There's a lot of work an architect has to do on a building before dump trucks appear at the **site**! First, they meet with **clients** to find out what the clients need and want for the building. Then, architects work with others to find a location and study the site. If adding onto an already existing building, that building is studied. Then, an architect drafts plans, or makes drawings using pens, pencils, and computers.

After the client approves all the details of the design, it's time to make the building happen!

Blueprints are plans made after a design has been approved. They have measurements and locations of walls, windows, pipes, electricity, and everything else that will be built. Models show what a design will look like when it's done.

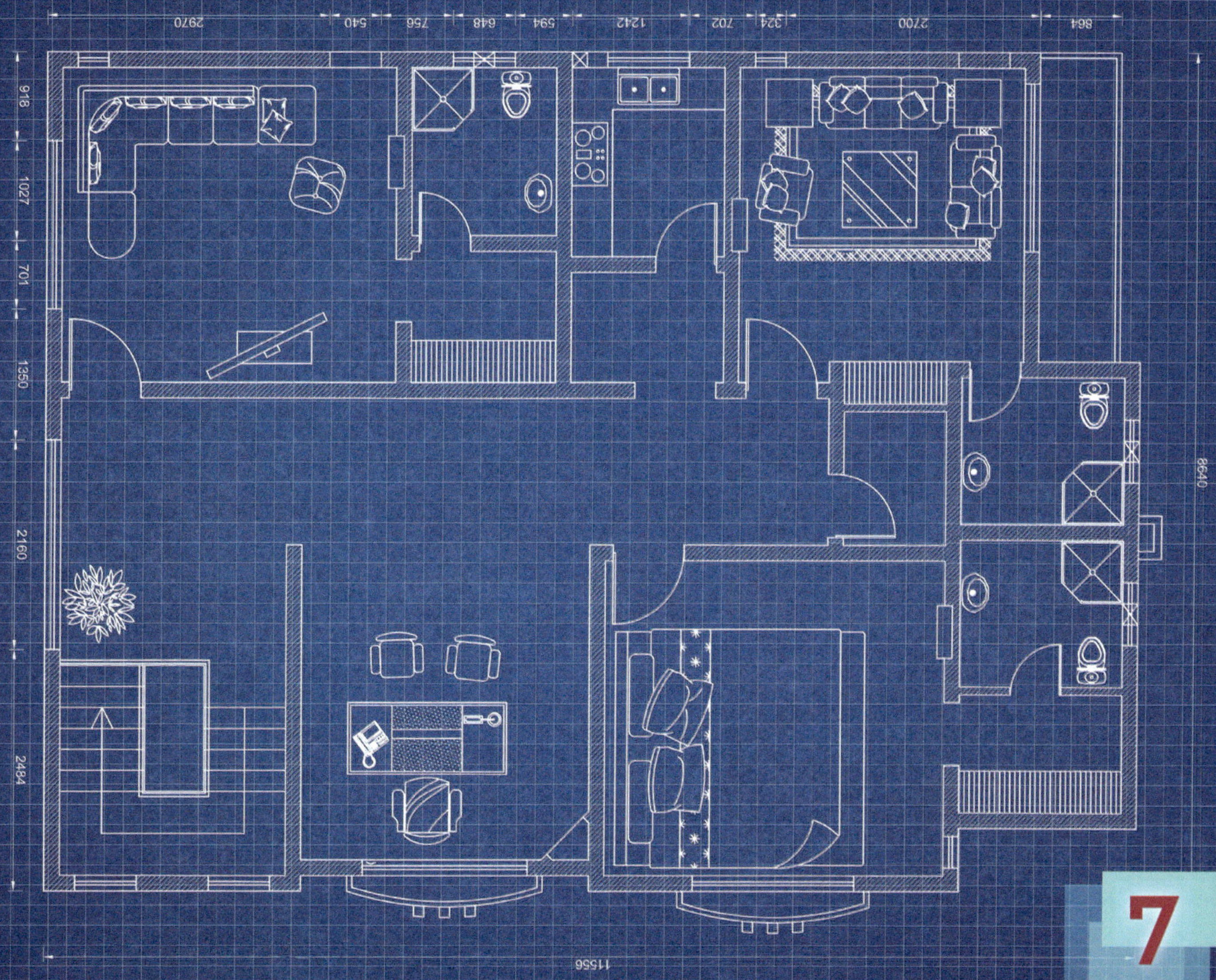

YOU DECIDE!

How exactly do you design a building? You have to make decisions about every single inch of it! An architect works with clients to decide the shape of the building, as well as the shapes of everything inside. They even consider what a building will feel like inside.

Architects also decide the building's **materials**. Buildings with many floors were once impossible! Many inventions such as sheet glass, steel, and **reinforced concrete** have made it possible to construct larger, taller buildings today.

TAKE A WALK!

Using scissors and paper, cut out a circle, half circle, rectangle, square, and triangle. Take a walk with an adult and your cut-out shapes. Do you see any of your shapes in the buildings you're walking past? Hold each shape out in front of you to see if you can find that shape in buildings.

Architects use materials and design to affect how a person feels inside a building. What do you think it feels like to be inside this building in Germany?

WHAT'S NEXT?

Designing is a small part of an architect's job. Mostly, they work with contractors, the people who oversee the building, to make sure everything's done right. Sometimes architects need to fix or change their plans when materials cost too much or it's taking too long to finish the **project**.

Architects are also in charge of getting the wiring, piping, and heating people organized and done with their work. A lot of this work takes place in their office, but sometimes architects have to visit the site.

WHERE HAVE YOU BEEN?

Architects design every room with a purpose, or function, in mind. List all the places you've been inside your school. Next to each place, list what you did there. Did the architect's design decisions make the room easy to use or hard? What rooms aren't designed well? What rooms are designed well?

Drawings that show the outside of a future building are called elevations. Elevations show windows, doors, porches, and other parts that belong on the outside of the building.

ALL THESE CHOICES!

With so many choices to make, how does an architect choose what shapes and materials to use—and how to use them? Many choices are affected by function. Function is how the building and each room will be used.

Choices are also affected by safety and cost. Certain materials and styles of design take less energy to build with and use less energy when the building's in use. For most projects, costs matter. Architects also make choices for a design based on the environment and weather of a site.

MAKE SHAPES!

You'll need a bag of mini marshmallows and a box of toothpicks. Using the marshmallows as connectors, make a square, rectangle, and cube. What other shapes do you see in architecture? Can you make a circle this way?

A kitchen's function is as a space to make food. Which of these kitchens looks easier to cook in? Why do you think each architect designed their kitchen the way they did?

WHAT DOES IT TAKE?

Architects need to be good at making choices. But what other skills do they need? Architects have to be organized enough to work on several projects at once. They have to be able to do math in their head all day long, which takes practice. They have to be good at problem solving.

Visualizing is very important for architects. This means seeing in their mind what a design will look like once it's built. It's important to help clients visualize by making great drafts and models.

BUILD A CASTLE

With an adult's help, look at pictures and drawings of castles on a computer. Gather leftover materials like paper rolls and cardboard boxes. Using tape to connect these recyclables, make a castle that includes design elements you observed!

Architects know how to talk to people, listen, and work together. They're also good at managing, or being in charge of, people.

BECOMING AN ARCHITECT

If you think you'd be a good architect, there are several steps to take before you can get to work! Since there's a lot of responsibility, architects must have 8 years of **experience**—including at least 5 years of **college**—before they can build!

In college, you'll take classes in math, architectural history, business, materials, design, and more. You may even travel with your college to study architecture! You'll probably also learn a lot about building in a way that's good for the environment, called green building.

DRAW YOUR HOUSE!

A floor plan is a draft that's made as if you're looking down into a house and the roof has been taken off. Each floor of a house has its own floor plan. Using graph paper and colored pencils, draw a floor plan of your home. Include windows, doors, furniture, and hallways!

In college, you'll learn how to design safe structures. A lot of safe design includes an understanding of **engineering**. Today, buildings can be engineered to better survive fires, terrible weather, and more!

AFTER COLLEGE

After college, you'll work for 3 years under a **licensed** architect to get real-world experience! This 5,600-hour period of work is called an internship.

Then, you'll need to pass a seven-part test, which usually takes 2 to 3 years. Once you've finished your education, internship, and testing, you apply for a license. You'll have to take certain classes every year or two in order to keep your license. The license only allows you to build in your state, so you need to apply for separate licenses to build in other states.

Most famous architects are from the past 500 years. Before that, only the name of the ruler who ordered the building was usually recorded. Going to school for architecture is pretty new, too! Architects used to study under another architect to learn. This is called apprenticing.

IS ARCHITECTURE FOR YOU?

Most architects work for architectural firms, which are groups of architects that all work together. But one in five architects owns their own company! Which do you think you'd like to do?

Architects do important work that's seen and used for many years. All kinds of buildings are needed in the world by all sorts of different people for a lot of functions. There are so many ways an architect can make a living. Do you love designing and finishing projects? Then maybe you should be an architect!

Designing your own house is a fun way to try out drafting for yourself. Do you want a video game room? A music room? Both? You get to decide!

DESIGN YOUR DREAM HOUSE!

YOU'LL NEED

- pencil
- graph paper
- ruler
- paper to write on

LEVEL 1

1. Make a list of rooms you'd want in your dream house.
2. Write down design ideas for each room, like furniture, windows, or even a water fountain.
3. Decide where rooms will go, remembering the function of the room. Don't put big windows in a movie room!
4. Decide where doors and hallways will go.
5. Draw your floor plan and label each room.
6. Erase parts of a wall line to make doors and windows, and label them.
7. Draw furniture, counters, sinks, pipes, and whatever else the room needs.

LEVEL 2

Draw the elevations, or outside views, of your dream house.

GLOSSARY

client: a person who pays a professional person or group for services

college: a school after high school

design: to plan and make decisions about something being created; also, the plans themselves

engineering: the use of science and math to build better objects

environment: the conditions that surround a living thing and affect the way it lives

experience: a chance to gain skills by doing something

landscaping: gardens, or the appearance of an area of land

licensed: having an official paper called a license that gives you permission to do, use, or have something

material: something used to make something, such as wood

project: a planned piece of work that has a specific goal

reinforced concrete: concrete that has metal bars inside it to make it stronger

responsible: having the job or duty of dealing with or taking care of something or someone; able to be trusted to do what is right or to do the things that are expected or required

site: the place where something (such as a building) is, was, or will be located

FOR MORE INFORMATION

Books

Jones, Rob Lloyd. *See Inside Famous Buildings*. London, UK: Usborne Publishing Ltd., 2009.

Tailfeather, Speck Lee, and Stella Gurney. *Architecture According to Pigeons*. New York, NY: Phaidon Press, 2013.

Viva, Frank. *Young Frank, Architect*. New York, NY: Museum of Modern Art, 2013.

Websites

Building Big
pbs.org/wgbh/buildingbig/
Learn all about how bridges, domes, skyscrapers, dams, and tunnels are built!

Pictures of Famous Structures
sciencekids.co.nz/pictures/structures.html
View pictures of famous buildings, structures, landmarks, and more!

Regional Chief Architect
kids.usa.gov/watch-videos/jobs/regional-chief-architect/index.shtml
Watch this video about Antonio Alonso, an architect for the US government.

Publisher's note to educators and parents: Our editors have carefully reviewed these websites to ensure that they are suitable for students. Many websites change frequently, however, and we cannot guarantee that a site's future contents will continue to meet our high standards of quality and educational value. Be advised that students should be closely supervised whenever they access the Internet.

INDEX